Freaks
of the Deep

Lisa Thompson

Blake
EDUCATION

C000124848

Brainwaves Blue
Freaks of the Deep
1 86509 923 6

Blake Education Pty Ltd
ABN 50 074 266 023
108 Main Rd
Clayton South VIC 3168
Ph: (03) 9558 4433
Fax: (03) 9558 5433
email: mail@blake.com.au
Visit our website: www.blake.com.au

Series publisher: Katy Pike
Series editors: Sophia Oravecz and Garda Turner
Designers: Matt Lin and Cliff Watt
Illustrators: Matt Lin and Aaron Lin

Picture credits: p14 APL/Minden Digital/Norbert Wu;
p16 Peter Batson/imagequestmarine.com; p17 (top)
Peter Herring/imagequestmarine.com; p18 APL/
MindenDigital/Norbert Wu; p23 photolibrary.com;
p24-25 Justin Marshall/imagequestmarine.com; p26
marinethemes.com/John Lewis.

Proudly printed in Australia by Printing Creations

CONTENTS

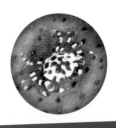

Dive into the Deep

You don't need to travel to outer space to see aliens. Just dive into the ocean.

Come see the strangest of creatures. One has lights all over its body. Another has a fishing line growing out of its nose. These are the freaks of the deep.

The Ocean Zones

Scientists have cut the ocean into zones.
Let's start at the top - in the sunlit zone.
90% of all sea creatures live here and
they're all hungry. Sea creatures have come
up with many ways to not get eaten.

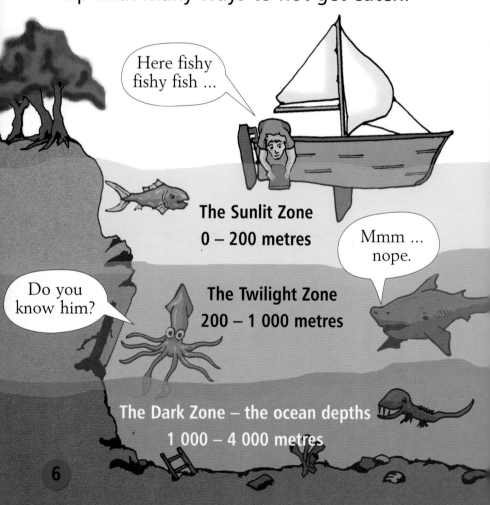

The Sunlit Zone
0 – 200 metres

The Twilight Zone
200 – 1 000 metres

The Dark Zone – the ocean depths
1 000 – 4 000 metres

Pretty Poison

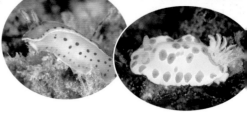

Some sea slugs are so bright; they almost glow in the dark. This is their way of saying, "I taste awful". Others are poisonous.

A sea slug is a kind of nudibranch. One group eats stinging coral. The nudibranch can then make the sting its own feathery weapon.

Warning! Stolen stingers inside.

Come on, touch me!

My tongue is as long as an elephant and my heart is as big as a car. Beat that!

All Puffed up

The puffer fish lives up to its name. When threatened, it gulps in water and puffs up into a spiky balloon. This makes it pretty hard to swallow. It's also very poisonous.

Fugu, very nice.

Wish me luck!

The puffer fish is called fugu in Japan. Fugu is eaten as a delicacy. The poisonous part is cut out very carefully before it is served. You just have to trust the chef as mistakes can be fatal!

Electric Shock

The catfish gives out a nasty shock. It zaps anyone who tries to eat it with an electric shock. The torpedo ray can also give you a jab of electricity. They're called stingrays for a good reason.

Hi Malina, zapped anyone today?

Not yet Ralph.

Touch an anemone and you'll get stung. But not the porcelain crab! It can hide safely within the tentacles and not get eaten.

Strange Shapes

It seems as if every shape is possible underwater. Think of the weirdest creature you can and you may find it under the waves. Many times the creature is just trying to hide, to blend in.

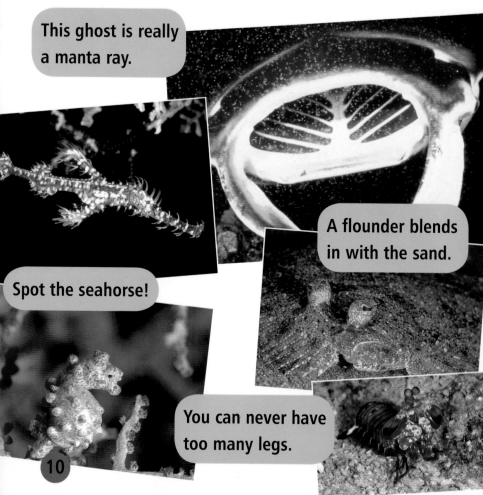

This ghost is really a manta ray.

A flounder blends in with the sand.

Spot the seahorse!

You can never have too many legs.

Gurnards creep along the sea floor using their three 'fingers'.

Look Mum, I can walk.

Hand fish and frog fish both have hand-shaped fins. The frog fish hops over the coral. The hand fish can rest on the sand.

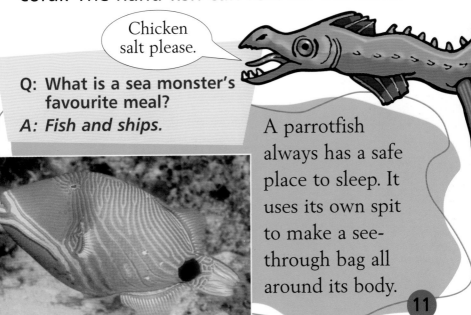

Chicken salt please.

Q: What is a sea monster's favourite meal?

A: Fish and ships.

A parrotfish always has a safe place to sleep. It uses its own spit to make a see-through bag all around its body.

Lights Please!

You are in the pitch black of the deep sea. You see a light. Do you go over and take a look? Or do you hide? Is it food or will you be eaten for lunch?

Here's trouble ...

Look at the pretty light. What do you think it is?

Not too sure Clarice. Should we go have a look?

Lighting up the Sea

Some creatures use their lights all the time. Others flash their lights on and off. Lights are used to attract food, see in the dark, or find a mate.

What a grin! Say cheese.

The anglerfish has its light at the end of a fishing pole. The **lure** on the top of its head lights up and attracts prey. When the prey comes close, the anglerfish strikes with a fast snap of its teeth.

Shrimp with lights on

lights?

Yes.

Bioluminescence

Most fish can't see the colour red, but a few can. Some deep-sea creatures produce a red light around their bodies that only they can see. The light lets these fish see and attack their prey, while they remain invisible.

A neon nudibranch

Switched on

"Down is on, right?"

The jewel-eyed squid is covered with small dots of light. These dots help it to hide. It makes the squid look like dappled sunlight. This protects it from predators. The squid can make the lights brighter or darker for different times of day or different **depths**.

The deep-sea glass squid rolls itself into a ball to protect itself.

"Fish breath is my protection!"

"My spikey ball is better!"

16

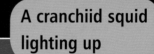
A cranchiid squid lighting up

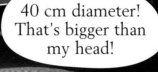
40 cm diameter! That's bigger than my head!

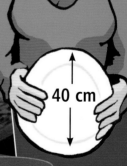
40 cm

Freaky Records
Largest squid's eye = 40 cm in diameter

Can You See How Pretty I Am?

Some fish use their lights to find their way. Others, like the viperfish, go around with their lights on. Why? They are hoping to find a mate!

Viperfish have teeth that are too big for their mouths.

I'm in love!

Hey! That's my girlfriend you're talking about!

The batfish uses its red lips to attract a mate.

I think brown is more your colour.

What about some nail polish?

These lights are just one of many strange **features** deep-sea creatures use to survive. Most special features are used to find food. And the deeper you go, the freakier they get!

I prefer chocolate myself.

Q: What fish tastes best with cream and ice-cream?

A: A jellyfish.

19

Freaky Features

Who are you calling weird-looking?

The deep sea has lots of water and not much life. Food may be a long time coming so you'd better be ready. You'll need eyes that grow as big as dinner plates to see in the dark, and huge mouths to catch a large dinner. And jaws that can flip open to fit it all in!

Errrr hi??

Big Biters

Many creatures that live in the inky dark have big eyes. Big eyes help them find food. They also have large jaws and teeth, for their small size. This means they can eat prey much bigger than they are. After all, with food hard to find, you don't want it getting away.

I want teeth like that.

There's lots of room for food in the mouth of an anglerfish.

Leave Room for Dessert!

The gulper eel has a large mouth. It can open it so wide that it makes a straight line! The eel swims along with its mouth open, ready to gobble up any food that it finds. It tips its head back and swallows fish whole.

The viperfish can move its organs around to make more room for dinner!

I think I might put my lungs behind my kidneys today.

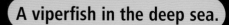

A viperfish in the deep sea.

Some deep-sea fish are red. In low light, red looks black.

I Spy With My Little Eye

When it gets really dark, eyes are no use at all. So down here most creatures have tiny eyes. Some don't even have eyes!

If you can't see, how do you find food? As the prey moves through the water, it makes waves that ripple outwards. The predator can feel this movement. Many fish hunt this way even when they can see.

The rodless anglerfish has tiny eyes.

You lookin' at me?

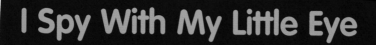

26

27

Chefs in Your Belly

Living next to a volcanic **vent** is hard. The water is boiling hot, and chemicals **gush** from the vents. Tube worms live in large groups around the vents.

A hydrothermal vent on the ocean floor

Don't know how you worms do it, it's so hot around here!

Tube worms live near hydrothermal vents.

A tube worm has no mouth, eyes or stomach. It's just a tube. The **bacteria** that live inside its body make the food. The bacteria change the chemicals from the vents into food. So, every worm has its very own bacteria chefs. Now how's that for freaky?

29

Fact File

Well I'm off to grow me a stomach.

Sea cucumbers can push out most of their insides to escape being eaten. They then crawl away and regrow their insides.

Sea spiders have tiny bodies and very long legs. They put some of their body organs down their legs.

The hagfish is a real monster of the sea. It covers its body with a thick slime that can kill other fish by clogging their gills. One hagfish can make enough slime to fill a milk carton.

Glossary

bacteria	tiny living things that can make you sick
bioluminescence	light that is made by animals
depths	deep down
features	special parts of something that make it different from others
gush	when lots of liquid comes out quickly
lure	a flap on the back fin of some fish
vent	a hole that gases or smoke come through

Index

What's a nudibranch?